BUILDING *Your* *Beauty* EMPIRE

The Ultimate Guide *to* Successfully Launch *Your* **Beautyprenuer Journey**

Lyndsey Brantley, *Medical Aesthetics Practitioner* and *CEO* of *Camellia Alise Inc.*

CONTENTS

*Y*our Success

Hi! I'm Lyndsey Brantley. I'm a wife, mother, writer, Beautyprenuer, teacher, and medical aesthetics practitioner with an unshakable faith and ambitious mission to help aspiring Beautyprenuers to successfully launch beauty brands.

*A **Beautyprenuer** is defined as one who organizes, operates, and/or owns a business that focuses its efforts on physically, spiritually, and emotionally beautifying their communities, via services and products.*

I come from a single-parent home, where we struggled daily just to have the basic necessities. However, my mom always found a way to provide for us one way or another. That humbling experience most certainly motivated me. When I went to college, I knew I wanted to make a better life for my family and show my mother how much I appreciated her sacrifice. The initial goal was to make a million dollars in corporate America once I earned my engineering degree. I had checked all the "boxes" necessary to pursue my millions, but after my first year in the oil and gas industry, I was laid off. This left me confused and searching for what would make me happy in my career. Eventually, I went through medical aesthetics training because I loved the spa industry and wanted to know more. I worked in a medical spa for an anesthesiologist and worked at a holistic spa at the same time. I became a sponge during that time. I learned everything I could about building a beauty empire: the skincare techniques, the systems, and the business side of the industry. I learned so much from both spa owners, who were powerhouses and amazing women, and I have carried those invaluable lessons with me.

I worked in both industries for more than eight years, gaining experience in aesthetics and using my engineering job to fund the aesthetics venture. When I was ready to have a family, I decided to go back into corporate America full-time because working both jobs was taking a toll on my body and mind. Simultaneously, I was struggling with my Polycystic Ovarian Syndrome (PCOS) and fertility treatments. During my first year back as a full-time engineer, I decided it was time to develop my own products and begin my Beautyprenuer journey.

For those of you who are unfamiliar with PCOS, it's a hormonal condition that some women endure during their childbearing years. It can affect your fertility, cause acne, irregular periods, weight gain, unwanted body and facial hair, and increase your risk of other health problems, including diabetes and high blood pressure. Personally, I was most affected by the body hair and skin sensitivity issues, so it inspired me to create a razor bump solution caused by the condition.

As a first-generation entrepreneur, I have made several mistakes along the way. But I have had just as many victories. I find freedom in being transparent about my journey. When I make an error, I can admit it and learn from it. In this book, I will share my experiences in hopes that I can prevent other Beautyprenuers from making some of those same mistakes. This journey has been beautiful yet stressful but worth it. I have been in boardrooms with Walmart executives pitching my ideas. I have won more than $50,000 in pitch and grant funds to launch my ventures. My company has been featured in several media outlets, such as *Essence, Ebony, The Huffington Post, Fox News* and many others. And while those honors have been a dream-come-true, my success all comes down to the plan, strategies, and visions I set for my business. We can all find success in this industry, and it is my hope that this book will arm you with the tools necessary to build a strong foundation for a successful launch in this industry.

"The worst they can say is 'No.'"

This is the motto by which I live. In life, we only get the things for which we aren't afraid to ask. If you are truly motivated to succeed, you will have to learn to find your home in uncomfortable moments in life and be brave enough to ask for what you really want. As a Beautyprenuer starting your journey, I intend to equip you with the tools you need to **eliminate excuses, execute efficiently, & enhance your enterprise by monetizing your expertise.**

I will expound on the three E's later in the book. For now, grab a pen, take notes and allow yourself to soak in the information in this book. It is meant to be a blueprint, but tailoring the information to your specific entrepreneurial needs is highly encouraged. Congratulations on making the first step to creating the Beautyprenuer life of your dreams.

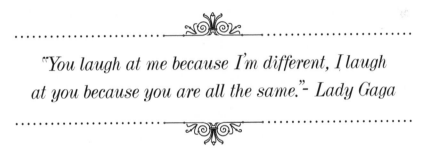

CHAPTER 1

$\mathcal{Y}$-our Niche- Defining who you are and what makes you special

---

"You laugh at me because I'm different, I laugh at you because you are all the same."- Lady Gaga

---

Every year, billions of dollars are spent in the beauty industry - from cosmetic and consumer products to beauty services including massages, body sculpting, esthetics and more. You have an opportunity to capitalize on these spending habits. You just need the right idea and systems in place.

What makes you different and what makes you stand out in this industry? These are the most important questions you will have to ask yourself as you build your brand. You see, no matter what product or service you create or market, there will always be someone who can create something

1

similar. It is up to you to establish what makes you unique and sets you apart.

Did you start your company for a cousin who has cancer? Were you tired of fighting dry skin? Did you lose your job and find your passion in a business venture?

When I first came up with the idea for skincare, I was simply going to create a body scrub and a lotion because everyone needs lotion, right? But why? Why did I want to create a lotion? What would make it different? I had to ask the same questions about creating a body scrub. What would be special about mine and why would a customer want to buy it over the next one on the shelf? I put great thought into these questions and found my answer. I wanted to create a scrub that would help get rid of my razor bumps. Women like me, who struggle with the effects of PCOS and hirsutism, deal with razor bumps more than the average woman. I identified a problem that I could solve and found my purpose behind creating those products.

A **niche** is defined as a distinct segment of a market and has a specific appeal. It is needed no matter what service or product you are offering. There are thousands of hair stylists and barbers out there, but my stylist specializes in healthy, natural hair growth. She is an expert in natural hair growth, and that is why I go to her for my haircare needs. What sets you apart?

In my experience, many beauty professionals dabble in several crafts before perfecting one specific skill. Many creatives struggle with this because they have an eye for variety. However, it is important to be an expert in what you are passionate about. If makeup is your passion, specialize in makeup.

If you are a nail artist who specializes in certain designs on the nails, then try perfecting and concentrating on just that. If you are passionate about natural skin care masks that slow the progression of wrinkles, there is a large clientele waiting for an esthetician just like you. There will always be clients looking for someone who specializes in your specific industry. All you have to do is reach out and market to your target audience.

To define your niche, make sure to follow these 3 steps:

STEP 1
Identify your consumer group

Make a list of the consumer groups that interest you, for example:

- Men or Women
- Moms
- Brides
- Strippers
- Corporate executives
- College students
- Cosmetologists

Think this through thoroughly. The more thought you give to your consumer group, the longer the list will become. Niche markets can be found amongst any group. They can be defined by physical features, hobbies, occupations, etc.

STEP 2
Identify products and pain points

Once you have your list of groups, think about the types of products they would use and/or problems they face or their pain points).

Product types:

- Skin moisturizer
- Sunblock
- Acne Cleansers
- Anti-Wrinkle Serums
- Makeup Wipes
- Hair Gel

Pain points:

- Vegan Preferences
- Gluten Allergies
- Paraben Issues
- Alcohol Sensitivities

This list could go on for forever, so try to limit your list to no more than 15.

STEP 3

Match up the who and the what

Now that you have your list of consumer groups and a list of products or pain points, just match them up. Some examples may be sunblock for male athletes or shampoo for bald men.

It's that simple.

Your specialty product is a good idea if there is a large enough market segment interested in buying it. Do your research to make sure the market is large enough to create a product for that target group.

CHAPTER 2

*Y*our Product Development- Private Labeling vs Custom Formulating

s I was writing this book, I watched the Netflix series "Self-Made", which features the life of Madam C.J. Walker, the first black female millionaire , she made her fortune by creating a line of hair products for black women. The series sets the scene for showing how Ms. Walker used her passion and love for helping women with their hair and confi - dence to build her beauty empire. She started from the humble beginnings of formulating products in her kitchen to owning a factory with several black women ambassadors and employees. Watching the series made me reflect on what it means to be a "Beautyprenuer". Being a Beautyprenuer can mean many different things for many different people. I, myself, have a custom formulated skincare line, a beauty school, and a brick and mortar spa. Perhaps, you are thinking about creating your own product or you are a full-time stylist, makeup artist, massage therapist, or esthetician. You fit the Beautyprenuer category no matter how your journey intersects with the beauty industry.

If you are thinking about entering the product development sector of the beauty industry, here are some tips and resources to help you successfully launch your line.

PRIVATE LABELING

Everyone does not necessarily start from scratch and put together their own list of ingredients, also known as an ingredient deck. Instead of going into a lab and developing your product from scratch, you can decide on the type of products that you want to bulk order and private label them. **Private labeling** is defined as products that are manufactured by a contract or third-party manufacturer and sold under a retailer's brand name. During the private label process, you will order samples, test out the products, try different scents, colors, etc. and determine what works for your product. By this point, you should have already identified your niche to make sure that the products match the brand you are trying to build. For example, if you want to have a vegan skincare company, do not use an ingredient with goat's milk or beeswax. After you choose the bulk products that work well for you, all you have to do is design your product labels, pick your jars, and you are ready to get started with few more steps in between, of course!

The companies I recommend reaching out to for haircare and skincare products are the following:

- Wholesalesupplyplus.com
- Wholesalenaturalbodycare.com

- Essentialwholesale.com
- Sourcevital.com

CUSTOM FORMULATED PRODUCTS

If you have a special ingredient, special purpose or an innovative product that is not available and you want to custom formulate it, here are the tips and resources to help you get started:

STEP 1

I highly recommend taking a class or two on formulation to better understand how to mix and match ingredients. Classes that can help you get started are:

- Formulabotanica.com
- Smartmajority.com
- Schoolofnaturalskincare.com

STEP 2

To get your ingredient deck together, here are the companies I recommend for raw ingredients:

- Bathbodysupply.com
- Texasnaturalsupply.com
- Brambleberry.com
- Rainshadowlabs.com

STEP 3

After you get a basic ingredient deck together, you need to find a manufacturer to help you test the product for safety, bacteria levels, shelf life, etc.

The companies I recommend starting with are:

- Texasbeautylabs.com
- Rainshadowlabs.com
- Mseed Labs

Before working with any manufacturer, check to be certain that the manufacturer is reputable and FDA compliant. The last thing you want is to have an amazing product that Walmart, Target or ULTA wants, but you can't get it certified in order to put it on their shelves! Make sure you have an NDA/ Confidentiality agreement signed (always protect your formulas). A confidentiality agreement is simply a contract be-tween two or more parties where the subject of the agreement is a promise that information conveyed will be maintained in secrecy. These agreements can be mutual agreements, where both parties are obligated to maintain secrecy, or they can be unilateral (one-sided) agreement, where only the receiving party becomes obligated to maintain secrecy. Also inquire, beforehand, about what the minimum order requirement is of the finished product and the costs associated with formulating. For example, some suppliers require that you order 500 ounces of your custom formula. If you are putting it in 4-ounce jars, that's 125 jars minimum. Other suppliers require you to order 30 or 50 jars of custom products. The minimum order quantity

(MOQ) changes depending on the manufacturer. Be sure to get this information before you begin the process, so you can budget for the initial order.

All the information I just provided you with comes from a hard lesson that I learned on my journey to product development. Here's my story. In March of 2013, I was so sick of battling with razor burn on my underarms, face and legs, and I was telling my friend about the frustrations. She simply said, "Create something to fix it!" Light bulb. From the day I started my company, I knew I wanted it to go beyond my kitchen for product formulation, but I also knew that's where I had to start. I mixed product ingredients and tested formulas for three years. Meanwhile, I was calling manufacturers and "interviewing them" and thinking about how to scale the products once I finalized the formulas. In January of 2016, I found my manufacturer. I was testing prototypes, and I thought I was ready to take the shaving and razor bump industry by storm. Little did I know, it wasn't about to happen - not that easily! My manufacturer at the time had a 500 oz. minimum, so I started making my scrubs first and utilized friends and family to test the products. I ordered jars and designed the labels and did all the things needed to launch. I got my final prototypes completed, won $10,000 in my first pitch contest for seed money (initial investment money), and I was ready to go. Just when I started selling the products and things were moving, disaster number one arose. Manufacturer "A" went out of business. It had taken more than six months to get them to recreate my formula and just as I'm ready to launch, I was forced to go back to the drawing board to find another manufacturer.

I tried starting the development phase with two other manufacturers, but I was unsuccessful due to cost for one manufacturer and capacity for the other. Three months later, I finally found the "right one." Manufacturer "B." We started the process on my first products, and they recreated the formulas. I created my new packaging and started selling products. I was so blessed that in just nine months from the time I launched, I landed a meeting to pitch my products to Walmart at their headquarters in Bentonville, Arkansas. But three weeks before I was scheduled to get on a plane for that pitch meeting, Manufacturer "B" called to tell me that the $50,000 mixer they used to create my scrub was now irreparably broken. This also meant they could no longer produce my shaving scrubs. Devastated was an understatement. What the hell was I supposed to do now? I was set to pitch this product to Walmart in three weeks! I began to feel like maybe it was not meant to be, and maybe this was a sign I should give up. But I didn't. ANY entrepreneur that you know who has achieved an ounce of success will tell you they did not get where they are with-out having moments where they wanted to give up. But that determination to reach my destiny would not let me do it. Fast forward to April 2017, I pitched for Walmart with my remaining products and I earned a deal to start selling on their online platform. During that time, I was looking for my next manufacturer. To be clear, I was always willing to quit my job and manufacture my own stuff out of my kitchen and garage if I had to! That's the sacrifice I was willing to make. Fortunately, I found Manufacturer "C." It took only six weeks for them to recreate my formula, and four years later, they are still amazing and producing my top-of-the-line products for me. I guess the third time *really* is a charm.

I told you this story to make these points:

- **In the moments when you want to give up, don't.**
- **ALWAYS be ready with a backup plan.**
- **Know your products and processes in and out because a journey that's truly worth it won't be easy.**

$\mathcal{S}$ervice Master- Owning your craft

L aunching your Beautyprenuer journey in the service industry means you're prepared to reach for the sky. This can be an exciting time that includes a roller coaster of emotions and accomplishments. Taking this leap will be risky. There's no way to avoid the risks, but the risks come with the potential for great rewards and success.

As a spa or salon owner, you can shape your business however you see fit. Depending on your cosmetic specialty, you may model your business around specific spa services such as massages, facials, and body contouring, or you may model the business around haircare services. No matter which service model your business chooses, there are a few things you need to consider in order to succeed.

Complete your niche cosmetology/beauty program. If you want to succeed in the beauty industry, you need to be professionally trained and accredited. The first step to take on your journey to success is to complete an educational program from an accredited and licensed institution. Without the proper licensing and certifications, you cannot legally practice, so do your research and know what your state requires to become a legit beauty service. Requirements on industry licenses and certifications are contingent upon state laws.

Begin building your portfolio. As a beauty service provider, you are an artist. Every artist needs a portfolio to show potential clients what they can do. Even a massage therapist needs small video clips and other imagery of their services. You will need a strong portfolio to attract clientele and show off your skills. It is never too early to get your portfolio started so as you are going through training, ask your clients and models if you can take before and after pictures of the services you provide. Also, utilize friends and family as a resource to build your portfolio. A wide and varied portfolio is a great advantage when seeking out your new clientele and showing off your skillset.

Start your career. Once you have your certification, don't procrastinate. Get started. You will have to make the decision of whether you want to work for a salon or spa or start the entrepreneurial journey on your own. Hopefully if you are reading this book it's because you want to go at it on your own. If that is the case, here are the tips I recommend to *own* your craft and go for it!

TIP 1
Take specialty classes and master your craft

Your education doesn't stop when you graduate from beauty school. One of the most amazing aspects of the beauty world is that it's always changing and growing, which means there is always something new to learn. Take the initiative to attend additional professional development and marketing classes. Marketing education is imperative to your business. Having a skillset and the *means* to market those skills to reach your target clientele are not the same thing. There are free or low-cost online and in-person workshop programs. There are also large conferences and beauty shows where you can learn about new techniques and products at reasonable prices.

The beauty industry is fast-moving and provides diverse opportunities for all types of practitioners. You may fantasize about becoming a beauty influencer. Your goal may be to have a full-service, million-dollar spa retreat. No matter your goal, you will need sufficient training to succeed in the industry.

TIP 2
Stand out in a crowded market

Listen to your customers, ask for customer feedback, and keep an eye on competitor activity, so you can stay ahead of the curve. My business recently sent a survey to customers asking how we could improve our products and what products our customers needed. We got the consistent request for a toner to go along with the razor bump products, so we formulated one and added it to the regimen. We regularly monitor the competitors in our industry - the larger companies such as Gillette and some smaller and growing companies like Get Bevel (both are now owned by Procter & Gamble). We watch the industry trends and find ways to stay ahead of them, largely by asking the customers what they want and need. We also differentiate ourselves by the audiences we serve. Some shave companies only market to women, or men, or specific demographics, like African American men. We also select a specific audience to market to and cater to that audience's needs.

DO CONSISTENT CUSTOMER RESEARCH

Part of your customer research should be an awareness of what's missing for local consumers. Identify the need and create your own stamp on the industry. Stand out from the other salons or spas in your area and make a difference.

Research can also be done through social media. Interact with people who offer a similar service to build your network and keep yourself in tune with the voice of your competitors. I work with spa owners all over the country to better understand what customers are asking for and what some of the latest services are. If you are a hairstylist you should follow other stylists online, "go live" with and direct message them and build your own network of specialist in your industry to learn from. If there is an exciting new product being introduced in New York that you think your customers in Colorado might like, ask the New York spa owners about it, and survey your clients. Always stay informed in your industry. The same works for the products or services that you *currently* offer. You don't have to constantly add new things. You can be extraordinary in what you are already doing and continue enhancing the experience. Do other stylists in your area offer champagne or foot soaks while clients are getting their hair done? Look for those small touches that add to the *experience* in your business.

While it's important to be aware of the industry trends, it is just as important to hear what your customers have to say and recalibrate based on their needs. There is nothing worse than a brand born out of simple market opportunity that doesn't pay attention to the customers' needs. Be authentic in who you are and what you are doing for your clients.

TIP 3
Build your professional community

Get to know other people who work in your industry. These are the people who will keep you informed about what's happening in your area. They can let you know about new jobs, educational opportunities, photo shoots, new product lines and more. Your network can help you cross-promote. If you're a bridal hair stylist or makeup artist, you should have a wedding photographer in your network. They can recommend you for potential jobs and vice versa.

"Your Network equals your Net worth"

TIP 4
Take advantage of the opportunities that come your way

It's important, especially when you're first launching your venture, to take full advantage of an opportunity when it arises. You never know where these opportunities may lead your business next. Some of the most career-defining moments come when you take a chance. These opportunities can be scary but can also push your career into a new and exciting direction!

A friend of mine, who is a nail artist, anticipated a lot of celebrities would be coming to Houston for the Super Bowl in 2017. She reached out to a bunch of her connections, and through her network, she landed the opportunity to do singer Lady Gaga's nails! She had already built her professional community and thus was able to create an opportunity for herself that was career-defining. Guess what? This would have never happened if she had not gone for it. Make sure that you seek opportunities but also create opportunities for yourself. Don't be afraid to ask around when you think certain opportunities may be within your reach.

TIP 5
Be knowledgeable on your selected beauty products

Your knowledge of your beauty products shouldn't stop with just the basic descriptions and features. Whether you are planning on working with a large volume of clients or an elite handful of them, there is going to come a time when clients will have questions about the products you use, recommend or sell. Clients are more willing to purchase from or seek a service from someone who is truly knowledgeable about their products.

No one expects you to know absolutely everything about all of your products. However, there are a few things you should know and be able to discuss with your clients.

- Do the products contain harmful chemicals?
- What is the reputation of the brand you are utilizing or promoting?
- What are the benefits of the product and why should the customer use it? Why do you choose to sell it?
- How will the product specifically help the client?
- Does the product company have a specific mission or social impact?

Always make sure the products you select are reasonably vetted.

TIP 6
Understand how to price your services

Being a Beautyprenuer does not require you to have a marketing degree, but that doesn't mean you shouldn't know basic business and marketing practices.

Research and compare your pricing with the prices being charged for similar services in your surrounding areas. Keep in mind that the results of the research should not be the sole deciding factor for setting your prices. You need to factor in your level of experience, education and training advantages, range of services offered, and service area availability to calculate what your fair and competitive pricing should be. NEVER be the lowest priced service or product in your area. With that in mind, you also shouldn't be charging so much that your clients feel taken advantage of or ultimately decide to go elsewhere because they can't afford you! Finding a great balance is key to growing and sustaining your clientele.

TIP 7
Be able to learn from correction and criticism

It doesn't matter how talented you are, there are going to be times when you get it wrong. You could be the best communicator on the planet, but miscommunications will still happen from time to time. When these things inevitably occur, it is important that you handle them with maturity and professionalism.

Mistakes are going to happen, and when they do it is vital that you address the issue, take responsibility and offer a solution. No one is suggesting that you let people treat you poorly or allow others to blame you for things you didn't do. It is simply important that when things don't go exactly the way you expected, you are able to pick yourself up, dust yourself off, re-evaluate and try again. This kind of cooperative attitude will be one of the qualities that allows you to gain the experience you will need for ultimate success.

When I first started my company, one of my mentors (who had a thriving beauty business) told me that my "Baby was ugly." Of course, I had to ask what that meant. She said my packaging was ugly. It was too dark, and you could barely see the words on it. She also said if it were on Target's store shelves, it wouldn't sell. Ouch. However, she had products selling well in retail, so instead of getting an attitude about her criticism, I listened to her suggestions. I went to several retail stores to compare the product labels and went back to the drawing board. It took 3 designs to get it right. Now, I am often complimented on how "store ready" my product labels are, but it took 2 failures and an honest mentor to get me there!

In the retail industry, we often deal with returns and customer complaints, as well. I once had a customer complain about and return a jar of scrub to Amazon because it did not have a double seal. There was a seal on the top inside but no plastic seal on the outside. Now if you are selling products on Amazon, you know that this is not a policy. You don't have to have 2 seals, but they will ALWAYS take the customer's side for returns. I could have looked at this as a silly complaint and moved on, but I didn't. I contacted the customer and added a second seal (a $.05 solution). She bought another one and 3 more after that because she appreciated the customer service. Over the last four years, there have been many situations like this. Most situations are small and easy to fix. They can either make or break your company and easily help you gain a loyal customer or gain negative reviews! Keep that in mind when you receive criticism or feedback on your business.

TIP 8

Be sensitive to your customers' mindsets and insecurities

As a service provider, clients will come to you for various reasons. There are a wide range of reasons that a client may self-conscious or insecure about their appearance. A person's self-esteem issues could come from any source or experience. Take the time to listen and observe your clients, so you can better assess their mindset and needs.

Listen when they tell you about themselves. An even more professional way to approach this is providing a quick consultation or client intake before getting started on their service. It is extremely important that you make every effort to be intuitive, sensitive, and receptive.

TIP 9

Always exercise creativity and innovation

Authentic enthusiasm can be infectious. If you are genuinely passionate about your business venture and journey, people will respond and be attracted to you. Inspiring and empowering others through your work attracts a wider audience and forges a deeper connection between you. This means that you need to make your passion for your work a priority.

Be creative by revisiting the things that inspire you the most about your chosen profession. Not only will this help you stay engaged with your profession, it may remind you of why you picked the profession and journey in the first place. Your clients and customers should never feel as though you dread working and interacting with them. If your clients feel this way, they won't be your clients for long. Be sure to give yourself time and space to find what you love about your Beautyprenuer journey and what inspires you the most.

Once you launch your venture, where you go and how much you achieve is entirely up to you. With these qualities in your arsenal, the sky's the limit.

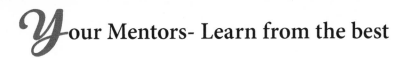

CHAPTER 4

*Y*our Mentors- Learn from the best

Throughout my entire entrepreneurial journey, I have always sought out and worked with mentors for guidance, advice and to ensure that my business succeeds. You should always have at least two to three mentors. Here are some of the categories of mentors:

- Industry Specific Mentor:

This is someone who has knowledge about the type of business you are in and has walked down a similar path. If you are a massage therapist, this mentor doesn't have to be another massage therapist, necessarily. A spa owner or similar service provider who has had to obtain and retain clients and build their business would be a great person to gain insight from as you build your venture. Be careful about how you approach these relationships because if the industries intersect too closely, the person may become defensive and see you as a competitor. It may serve you best to find a mentor that lives outside of your immediate target area. A burger restaurant owner opening a location in Dallas probably shouldn't ask another burger restaurant owner in Dallas for advice. It may be best for that owner to ask advice of a burger restaurant owner in Atlanta or a place with a similar demographic.

- Non-Industry Specific Business Leader:

Connect with a person in a different industry that you admire. As a Beautyprenuer, you may choose to form an entrepreneurial relationship with a leader in the food, hospitality or even the auto industry. They can offer you a different perspective, so that you will have diversity and innovation in your plan.

- General Business Mentor:

This is someone who can help you with growth and development in certain areas of your business. This is perhaps someone with a legal background or financial background. This may also be a general business owner who is established, knowledgeable and someone you respect.

As a Beautyprenuer, there will be many days where you will encounter unchartered territory in your business or days when you will need a little extra encouragement. You will need people around you who can help you move past those difficult moments. In a typical business mentoring relationship, an experienced business owner will meet with a new business owner one-on-one and will give them advice and help boost their morale. Having a business mentor in your corner is crucial to your survival in entrepreneurship.

The top 7 benefits I have found in having a mentor are:

1. Receiving valuable advice

The greatest benefit to having business mentors is being able to ask questions and leverage the mentors' experience to get valuable advice. As a new business owner, it is not wise to get advice from friends and family, especially if they have no experience in your industry or as an entrepreneur. Having an unbiased opinion is a great thing and can provide a new perspective for problems and unanticipated situations.

2. Improving critical skills

Mentors are not like advisers and consultants who care only about the business venture. Instead, business mentors help you develop your personal business skills. For example, if your employees are constantly complaining that they don't understand project directions, your business mentor can work with you to help you improve upon how you communicate with your staff.

3. Having a trustworthy sounding board

Owning a business can be stressful and frustrating. You will definitely need to vent to someone you can trust and talk things through when times get tough. Do not vent to your employees or customers, as this can create an unstable business structure. If you are always whining to customers, they will eventually stop coming to you, or they will think something is wrong with the business. People are often repelled by negative energy. The same is true for employees. Let's say you complain about "not making enough money" to your employees. They will think there is no longevity in your business, so they will eventually leave. If you often criticize customer feedback or complaints, the morale for the customers will go down. In turn, your employees may become disrespectful to your customers. It is a negative domino effect. You run the same risk if you constantly use your partners or investors as a sounding board. Someone who invests in your company believes in you and your vision and thinks you know what you are doing. When you complain to investors, they may lose faith in you and your ability to effectively run and grow your company. However, once you vent and express your frustrations to your *mentor*, you can actually start the process of working through the issues that are causing your frustrations.

4. Expanding your network

Business mentors often connect you with contacts who can help your business grow and flourish. The more networking you do, the more knowledge you will gain on industry trends. This means more access to resources needed to further your business, create opportunities, and share information.

5. Methods and execution strategies

In addition to giving advice and helping improve your personal business skills, business mentors can offer you methods and strategies that you can build you up throughout your journey as a business owner. If you are looking to increase sales, who better to ask than a retired business owner who ran and operated a brick and mortar business for 30 years?

6. Stretching your limitations

Starting a business can be difficult, an d many business owners face challenges early in the process. However, you are not alone and many of the issues you face are not new to other business owners. Hearing first-hand from your mentor about their experiences and how they overcame some of the same issues you are facing can help you to become a better entrepreneur and inspire you to push further than you normally would have without that little nudge of confidence.

7. Opportunity to create a win-win relationship

Mentees are not the only ones who benefit from business mentoring. Business mentors also experience benefits thanks to collaborative learning. By helping others improve their business skills, business mentors may enhance their own skills. They may be inspired with new ideas, meet new contacts and learn new business strategies from their mentees.

When seeking out a mentor, look for people who are near you, know you and have an understanding of what you are trying to achieve with your business venture. That's the best way to find a person who will truly be invested in your journey and your success.

Also remember to use your local resources to seek out mentors. There are local chapters of SCORE (Service Corps of Retired Executives), SBDC (Small Business Development Center), community colleges, and other national organizations that are geared toward providing small business owners with mentors in all industries.

When I was a year into my business, I was blessed with the amazing opportunity to be briefly mentored by Lisa Price, founder and creator of Carol's Daughter, a haircare line for natural women. One day, she was at a local H-E-B grocery store introducing a new collection, and something came over me. I mustered up all the courage I had and walked up to her, offered her a sample of one of my products and asked her to be my mentor on the spot! It just happened to be the right time and place because she said, "Yes." If ideal situations present themselves, go for it. However, I caution you not to be overly aggressive in the moment because every person is different when approached by strangers asking for help. Thankfully, it worked out for me. If I never asked her, I would have missed out on a really great opportunity!

When you have the chance to be mentored by a trailblazing CEO of her caliber, you typically have a limited amount of time to spend with them. You *must* be ready to capitalize on that opportunity, so have a list of questions ready to go and be ready for the conversation. Avoid wasting their time by asking superficial questions like "What do you do?" or "How did you get started?" You should have already done research on them and answered these basic questions about them well in advance.

Here are the 25 questions I recommend starting with if you get the opportunity to be mentored by or have a conversation with a top industry leader in your field. Of course, you can tailor the questions depending on the objective of the call, time allotted, and with whom you are speaking.

- What would you do if you were in my position, starting in today's business climate?
- How would suggest obtaining new clientele and a following (social media, local shows, going for the big box stores etc.)? Where would you recommend, I start?
- How long was it before you outsourced some of your business logistics, such as bottle filling, labeling jars, virtual assisting, etc.?
- Where did you envision yourself when you first started? Is this where you thought you would end up?
- How did you earn your first celebrity endorsement?
- What was one of your biggest weakness, and how did you overcome it?
- What would you do differently in your business?
- What was your initial investment in your company and yourself?
- With whom (people/brand/organizations) do you recommend I get connected?
- What are you most proud of from your journey?
- What professional organizations are you associated with and in what capacities?

- What do you wish you had known at my stage of business?
- *Why* do you do what you do?
- What do you still struggle with in business?
- How do you currently spend your time? What's next for you?
- What things do you consider when planning for the future? What are some of the things I should consider in my planning strategy for the next 12 months?
- What's one thing you wished people asked you more often?
- What qualities do you look for in a mentor?
- How do you approach the unknown?
- What was your first sales pitch like?
- What books or resources should I read to grow personally or professionally?
- What was the biggest risk, or leap of faith you took while starting your business?
- How did you obtain investors and at what stage did you seek out help?
- How can I return the favor? I am so appreciative of your time and want to enrich your life as much as you will enrich mine because I so blessed to have this opportunity!
- How would you like me to follow up with you?

$\mathcal{Y}$our Marketing Essentials

WEBSITES

One of the most effective ways to promote your beauty brand is to put it on the web and begin developing your online reputation. Almost all your potential consumers or clients are searching and shopping online. Make sure to have an e-commerce website that is smartly designed and includes all the relevant information such as product and service descriptions, prices, benefits, and other features. Also make sure that your website contains your contact information including a phone number, email and physical address. Your e-commerce site should resonate with your target customers and draw their attention.

Determine which platform you want to use to build your website. I highly recommend platforms such as:

- Shopify
- Magento
- Wix

WordPress is also a great platform, but I found that it is not for the "amateur" website builder and works better if you have a graphic designer who will build the site for you!

"SEO" SEARCH ENGINE OPTIMIZATION

"SEO" Search Engine Optimization is the process of getting traffic from the "free," "organic," "editorial" or "natural" search results on search engines. Here is why SEO is so important. If you go to Google and search "Spa Houston" or "anti-wrinkle solution," you are 95% more likely to call, click on, or explore the spas or products that show up on the first page of your Google search. You want your business in that top spot or as close to it as possible. Nowadays, it's not enough to simply have a business website. You need to have your business and product/service listed on Google, Yelp, Amazon or Etsy, and on social media. Determining which sites you are listed on depends on the type of beauty business you are launching. If you are service based, you should create a Yelp account where your customers can check in and rate you, which increases your visibility. If you have a product business, Google Merchant can drive your page to the top of your category much faster than just having a Google business page alone. Of course, it's not mandatory to list and sale the products on Amazon or Etsy, but research has shown that Google uses those additional listings to build your SEO credibility as well!

Below are two images that show the difference in what a general skincare search would look like. Statistics show you are

65% more likely to click on one of the images on the Google Merchant pop up. It's all about grabbing your potential customers' attention. The more people who see what you offer, the more people you can sell to!!!

vs

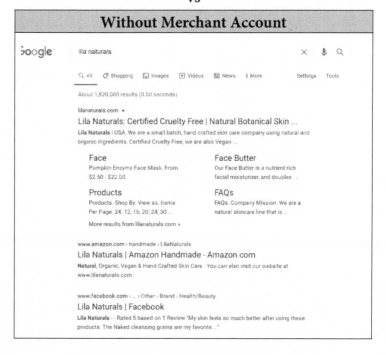

SOCIAL MEDIA

Social mediums including Instagram, Facebook, Twitter and YouTube are optimum marketplaces to sell your beauty products and services aggressively. These virtual markets help you to increase your reach to potential consumers. All you need to do is post interesting content and visuals regularly to create a dominating presence. If you have Facebook, make sure to take advantage of the shopping page capabilities. Take some time to connect your website to Instagram, so you can directly tag products as you post them.

Lastly, when you are posting content on your virtual markets, make sure it is relevant, entertaining, and authentic. Show the products you are selling. Show photos and videos of clients you are servicing. Offer tips to which your target audience can relate. If you are selling a hair product or service that will help your client's hair grow, post before and after photos, as well as tips and techniques that encourage hair growth. You can gain leverage with this content because you know this is a subject your clients/targeted audience will be interested in learning about. This will definitely increase engagement and prompt more discussions on your page.

DISTRIBUTE FLYERS AND BROCHURES

Your printed business materials should be a single sheet (front and back) that includes your product or service images, products and services descriptions, and your company's contact details. The cost of creating a flyer design is the most cost-effective in comparison to other marketing materials. A good price-range for design is about $20 to $60 per flyer design. Use graphic designers from companies such as:

- Upwork.com
- Fiverr.com
- Peoplebythehour.com

Once you have the printed materials on hand, use them at any vending events and partner with local vendors who can also sell your products. You should also consider using the flyers or brochures as mailers to send to potential customers in close vicinity to your business. You will also need marketing materials such as business cards and logos to make a good impression on the potential customer. The companies listed above can also design these items for your business.

OFFER SEASONAL AND INTRODUCTION DEALS

People will always be attracted to sales and offers that are enticing to them. For example, if you're starting a product company, you can offer introductory discounts to motivate customers to try the products. The same works very well with services, especially ones that need to be bought in packages or sets.

Think about offering deals such as, "Buy One, Get One Free" or giving a gift with first-time purchases. You should also consider running seasonal deals for Black Friday, New Year's, Fourth of July, and other major holidays or seasons.

My biggest sale to date has been a "Black Friday" sale that I offered for services. Typically, I give a 10% or 15% discount on items, but during that time, I offered a package of 6 services for 45% off. I made more than $10,000 is sales in one day! The sale went on for 2 weeks, and I got amazing results. I attribute the sale's success to how it was packaged. Instead of making $129 for one service, I was making $450 per customer and guaranteeing that they would come into the spa multiple times for services.

GET TESTIMONIALS AND FEEDBACK

Referrals and word-of-mouth are the best advertisement. A testimonial is one of the most powerful influences in a customer's decision-making process. Shorten your potential customers' research process by providing the testimonials related to your product. Testimonials are great, but you will never know if something is wrong or what needs to be improved upon if you don't ask! With that in mind, it's extremely important to get your customers' feedback, as well. If you are launching something new, you have to find out what the customers like and dislike about the products or services, so you can quickly improve them if needed.

Use companies such as surveymonkey.com, jot form. com, or Google docs to create a quick 10-question survey. Incentivize your customers by giving them a small discount on their next order for answering the questions! It's a win-win for both parties.

CONTENT MARKETING

Content marketing is one of the most powerful strategies when it comes to brand recognition. It's all about distributing relevant and valuable content to attract, acquire and engage your target audience.

Make sure you use the following to engage your audience and create valuable content:

- Create "how-to" videos to teach people how to use your products, what the benefits are and why they should choose it.
- Build a newsletter subscriber list and use it to send out special promotions and engaging content to your existing and potential customers.
- Participate in "live" video broadcasts to interact with your clients in real-time on social media. Video content is highly engaging; therefore, it is an easy way to help boost organic audience interaction and reach consumers for free. If you are like me and do not like to do live videos, a podcast or an alternative video format may also be extremely useful.
- Interview people from your industry. Reach out to bloggers, influencers, and other experts in your field who are engaging and have a following. If you are a stylist, there are tons of other stylists you can work with to help engage your audience on specific topics. This can be a true reciprocal strategy for you both.

COLLABORATE WITH INDUSTRY-RELATED PROFESSIONALS

Create a holistic approach to beauty by partnering with other brands and companies in other related industries. If you are launching a haircare product, find barbers and salons to carry your products. If it's a skincare line, find spas to carry your products. This strategy can be applied to a service-based business, as well. If you are launching a body contouring business, you can partner with personal trainers to widen your clientele base. These beneficial partnerships help build brand trust and credibility. It also opens new distribution channels.

SOCIAL MEDIA INTERACTION

You should be posting on your social media channels a minimum of 7 times per week. Posting up to 3 times a day is optimal to keep your audiences engaged. Here are a couple of ways to keep new ideas coming for content:

- Publish "Scroll Stopping" Instagramable content. If you don't have a huge budget, consider collaborating with talented amateur photographers.
- Publish "before and after" stories to prove the effectiveness of your products or service.
- Collaborate with aspiring beauty influencers or service providers to attract new prospects.
- Analyze popular hashtags in your beauty niche using IQ Hashtags, then easily plan, manage and schedule

your communication with social media posting apps/ sites such as, <u>Planoly, Later.com, Hootsuite, or Buffer.</u>

- Offer a free giveaway contest to get people sharing and tagging their friends to your page.
- Stay positive, engaged, and customer centric. Respond quickly and in a friendly way to customer feedback or questions. Placing your audience's needs first keeps them coming back for more!

In the highly competitive beauty and cosmetics market, simply owning a natural beauty brand or service is not enough anymore. You'll have to work hard to tell your unique story and to make sure the right audience is exposed to it.

$\mathcal{B}$uilding Your Team

I can, under no circumstances, say that I built my business on my own. There is no way I could be writing this book or having a thriving business today without help. When I started my business, I was mixing skincare products in my kitchen with family members who helped to bottle, label and ship orders, while I focused on marketing and customer feedback to ensure that the products worked well. I initially had an informal partnership with someone who contributed financially but as the business grew, we found ourselves at an impasse on the path forward. I eventually bought her out to gain complete ownership of the company again and moved forward on my own. Six months later, I hired my first marketing consultant who helped to increase my network. However, within 2 months of working with me she was asking for equity and a COO position based on a promise that she would take the company far. Needless to say, I had to walk away from that business relationship, as well.

As a startup entrepreneur, getting the right team together will always be a challenge. I can personally attest that there is definitely a right and a wrong way to grow your team. In the beginning, hiring the right people is essential because your employees become your brand and allow your customers, investors, and other potential employees to see what kind of company you are building. Here are some of the major tips I have learned along the way:

TIP #1
Set the expectation from the beginning.

As you start your business, think about how you want to do things to make your business a success. Then start doing those things right from the beginning. Start the race how you want to finish it. It will always be easier to start tough and lighten up than to do the opposite. With that same mindset, you must start with high expectations for employees. Expect a lot from people you hire, including freelancers, and let them go quickly if they do not meet expectations within a proper timeframe. My number 1 mistake was holding on to employees too long when I knew I needed to let them go for the sake of my business.

Here's an example. Jennifer has a cookie delivery business. She hired Sheila as a driver to take on some of the delivery jobs that did not fit her schedule. Upon hiring her, Jennifer told Sheila, "I want you at the client's door 5 minutes before the expected delivery time. EVERY TIME. I tell my customers that we will be early every time, and that is the customer service excellence they expect. If you are late just once, I will have to fire you." Sheila was five minutes early the first day, but she was seven minutes late the second time. The client complained and asked for a discount on their next order. Consequently, Jennifer fired Sheila. Was that too harsh? She could have given her another chance, but she did not want to have to deal with lateness. Sheila also didn't communicate that she would be late, and it was only day two! Jennifer knew she had to start her business out the way she intended to maintain it, and tardiness was a non-negotiable.

Why is starting with clear expectations so important? It's all about starting with good habits. If you already have a business and have some bad habits or low expectations, have you noticed that those business traits have trickled down to your employees' performance? It will take some effort, but you can turn things around. It is certainly worth the effort to get back to where you need to be.

Be thoughtful about how you want to do business. You don't have to have a 10-page employee manual, but you need an established way of working and clearly communicate it to your employees from the day they come in to interview with you.

Whenever situations arise that could be a problem, stop and decide how it should be dealt with each time. Make it a rule for you and your team to adhere to and clearly communicate it to them.

Tip #2
Put it in writing.

Clear job descriptions are a must! The description you put out there is your chance to make a good first impression as a hiring company. Start thinking about the unique characteristics that make your company appealing. The type of job description you publish is closely related to who you are as an employer. Give your potential employees a glimpse of your company that will charm them into applying and wanting to come to work for you. Candidates must be able to relate to job descriptions on a personal level. Tell them a story about your company that will make them sit back and picture themselves working with you. Ask current employees why they enjoy working with you and use that feedback to build your descriptions.

Tip #3
Look for characteristics that cannot be taught.

You can teach financial analysis or how to interpret Facebook Analytics reports, but it is much more difficult to teach an adult proper manners, ethics, or expertise. Skills and experience are worthless when not put to proper use. Knowledge is also useless when not shared with others. The smaller your business, the more likely you are to be an expert in your field, so look for people who have the specific characteristics that you may lack. For example, I'm an amazing researcher and product formulator, but I'm an introvert. I look for outgoing employees who love relationship building and networking to grow my company in a way that I may not be able to because of my reserved personality.

Bonus Tip: Carry out behavioral interviews, in addition to the standard ones. Have the applicants fill out the Myers Briggs personality test from sites like https://www.16personalities. com/ . If a potential employee is going to be your receptionist, they should definitely be an extrovert or letter "E" personality, first. Keep in mind, many new hire failures are due to lack of motivation, an unwillingness to be coached, or problems with temperament and emotional intelligence!

TIP #4
Everyone signs a confidentiality agreement.

When building your business, it is vital that you have *every employee* sign a confidentiality agreement before they start working for you. Starting your business is not an effortless thing, and it certainly wasn't easy coming up with your ideas, formulas, techniques, products, systems, etc. The last thing you want is an employee to come in and take your ideas with no recourse or protective measures in place. Keep in mind that as an entrepreneur, you are taking an idea and turning it into a profitable enterprise. By all means, you need to protect your ideas by having confidentiality agreements with non-disclosure provisions in place.

CHAPTER 7

Your Business Plan

I wrote my first "skeleton" business plan back in 2013 when I first came up with my skincare idea. It was four pages long, and I had no idea what I was doing! It included what I was going to sell, who I was going to sell it to, how much I wanted to make in the first three years, and how I was going to sell it. It was really just something simple, but I knew I needed to write down my goals and what I wanted to do. It wasn't until 2015 when I started taking classes at the SBDC - Small Business Development Center- that I learned all the elements needed for a business plan and got a mentor to help me start to build it.

In 2016, I joined the City of Houston's Lift Off Business Plan competition, which is a 6-week plan designed for startup businesses to build an "Investment Ready" Business Plan. Ultimately, I won that competition. Here is what I learned that helped me to win that competition and garner later investments.

The key elements for your business plan are:

- Executive Summary (Fill out this part last!)- All of the other components of your business plan will help you to formulate a powerful executive summary.
- Industry Overview
- Product/Service Descriptions
- Market Strategy & Target Market
- Competitors
- Business Strategy & SWOT Analysis
- Organization & Operations
- Financial Plan
- Proposed Financing and Usage of Funds

Each of these elements is a *must* if you are planning to seek investments into your startup business. Even if you aren't looking for investors, I always refer to the saying, "If you don't know where you are going, you'll end up someplace else." As an entrepreneur you may need to pivot when new circumstances arise, but it's essential to have a foundation to begin with so you know where you are trying to go!

Here are the basic questions that you need to answer in each of these sections. Keep in mind that your total business plan doesn't need to be more than 30-35 pages. Also, the plans written down don't have to be concrete. Your plan will continue to evolve over time with your business development.

1. Executive Summary

- What is the business and the corresponding business concept?

- What is the opportunity and the basic strategy to take advantage of the opportunity?
- Why will the company be successful?
- What is the target market?
- What are the competitive advantages of the business concept?
- What is the team that will be required to start and sustain this business?
- Why you are uniquely qualified or motivated to lead this company?
- What will the return on investment be for prospective investors?

2. Industry Overview

- In what industry will the business compete? Describe in terms of products/services.
- What is the business and its concept?
- What products and/or services will it offer?
- How will the business enter this industry and how will it grow?

3. Product/Service Descriptions

- What is the product/service you are introducing to the market?
- What are the benefits & features of the product/service?
- What is unique or innovative about it?

4. Market Strategy

- In what market will the business compete?
- Who is your target audience/consumer?
- How will product/service be positioned, priced, and packaged?
- Who will you sale to? B2B(Business to business), B2C (Business to consumer), etc.
- What distribution channels will be used?
- What special marketing strategies will be employed, including promotions, samples, or discounting deals?

5. Competitors

- Who are your competitors in this industry?
- How will your product/service differ from them?

6. Business Strategy

- Describe the business model including projections of revenues, margins, profits, and break even.
- What is the overall schedule from start-up to profitability?

7. Organization and Operations

- What is the company's organizational and legal structure?
- How will the product/service be designed and developed? By whom?
- What design/development costs are expected?

- Are there any design/development proprietary issues, e.g. licensing?
- What is the manufacturing and/or operations plan, including facilities, location, and ramp up?
- What key team members are needed for the company to succeed?
- Will you need outside experts, consultants, and advisers?

8. The Financial Plan

- Income projections (three years)
- Balance sheets (three years)
- Cash flow Projections (three years)
- Break even calculations

9. Proposed financing and fund usage

- What financing will be needed to fund the business?
- What sources of capital will be used?
- How will invested funds be utilized?
- What is the return on investment to potential investors (three years)?

If you need examples of business plans to start with you can go to the following websites for templates:

- Bplans.com
- Sba.gov
- Profitableventure.com/beauty-salon-business-plan/
- Score.org

CHAPTER 8

*Y*our Funding

In today's climate and due to some of the recent changes with the COVID-19 pandemic, it's probably easier than ever to obtain an SBA loan than if you started your business before the pandemic hit. It's easier now because the focal point for the country has been to get the economy back on its feet and billions of dollars have been approved by the government to help with the process. Traditional banks have relaxed some of the standards they normally have for loans, are accepting lower credit scores and are more willing to take risks on startup businesses. The loan rates have decreases as well.

If you are trying to start up your business from scratch, you should have a plan to get some funding for the business. Even if you have money set aside, I recommend that you try obtaining money before you *need* it. More often than not, the moment that you need money, no one will want to give it to you! Nearly 45% of my business was funded with money from pitch contests and grants that I didn't have to pay back. Below I will share some of those competitions with you, but I say this to say, there is definitely money out there. You just have to look for it and apply. I didn't actually get a business loan until I was three years into the business with staff and a brick and mortar spa. At this point, I wanted to obtain the loan to expand my staff and marketing efforts for growth. But until year three, it was pitch contest funds and my own money that helped me get started.

Before you start your business, you need to know how much money you need to obtain and start finding ways to get the money. Some alternative ways to get funding would be:

- Crowdfunding platforms such as:
    o Ifundwomen
    o Kickstarter
    o Indigogo
    o NextSeed

Crowdfunding is a method of raising capital through the collective effort of friends, family, customers, and individual investors and does not need to be paid back!

- Pitch contest. Look for local ones in your area but here are some of the Houston-based and national competitions of which I am aware:

    o New Voices Fund
    o Houston Liftoff competition
    o HCC business plan competition
    o Next Seed Female Founders
    o Bank of America
    o BBVA Compass

o Cricket Wireless

o HMSDC

Pitch contests are dedicated programs which give people an opportunity to pitch their idea to a group of investors and industry experts. They have rules for eligibility, panels of judges, workshops that strengthen the entrepreneur's skills, and typically, the competition focuses on awarding capital and opportunity to entrepreneurs.

- Applying for grants is also a way to score cash for your business. Here's a few:

  o Grants.gov
  o Local and industry-related organizations (grant programs are everchanging)

A business grant is a sum of money given to a business in order to help them further their business. They're usually distributed by governments, corporations, foundations, or trusts. Unlike many other types of business funding, grants don't have to be paid back and business owners aren't required to give up equity in exchange for a grant.

If none of these options work and you need alternative lending (as big banks rarely fund startups,) I recommend you start with the companies below that fund startup ventures.

- Alternative lending:
  o Trufund
  o Peopefund
  o Liftfund

CHAPTER 9

*Y*ou shouldn't quit your day job!!

T his can be a very touchy subject depending on who you talk to about entrepreneurship. There are some people who are of the opinion that you aren't a "real" entrepreneur unless you jump head-first into the business. Because of my experience, I am not one of those people. If you happen to find yourself in a place where you have no choice, that is a completely different situation. I know many successful entrepreneurs who were laid off or found themselves unemployed due to unforeseen circumstances, so they went full force into the business. This has paid off greatly for them. If that is your situation, I say, "Go for it!" But if you have a job and you have a burning desire to launch your beauty empire, plan a strategic exit and be wise about when you want to move into full-time entrepreneurship. I fully respect and admire people who go into their business fulltime, but during my first year in business, my paycheck was the only thing that kept the products on the shelves and the doors open. When I was custom formulating and researching, it took a lot of time and initial investment to get the ingredients and branding right. In other words, I needed my job to fund the dream. If you can strategically get to a place where you can replace your income, I recommend you do it. Better yet, plan and save enough before you launch, so you can afford to live on the savings your first year running your business full-time. Whichever way you choose to launch your Beautyprenuer journey, the most important thing to do is plan!

Here are a few specifics to consider before transitioning fulltime into entrepreneurship:

Have some funds intact. It can take months before you get your first sale or you gain any traction in your chosen industry, so you need to have at least six months' worth of living expenses available to replace the regular paychecks you have been earning.

Have your plan ready. You need to set some short-term and long-terms goals to accomplish and be committed to accomplishing them in order to keep yourself going and encouraged as you transition. Make a list of at least 4 goals to accomplish in 30 days, 4 goals to accomplish in 60 days, 4 goals to accomplish in 90 days, so forth and so on. Plan your business out as efficiently and clearly as possible, so you know what you want to achieve. Check the list each month and modify the goals as needed but use them as a calibration map to keep you focused.

Mentally and physically prepare for the stress ahead. Many aspiring entrepreneurs underestimate the amount of pressure that will be placed on them to perform, meet deadlines, meet sales goals, and be able to rise in moments of crisis and failures. As you begin your transition, you should have a coping mechanism or two already in place to help you through these moments. I personally meditate and take daily walks, amongst other things, to help cope with mine.

Test your idea for market traction. The last thing you want to do is transition full-time to sell a product or service that no one is buying. It is best to test the idea first. Start offering the prod-uct or service at local events or online and get initial feedback before you jump head-first into it.

Strengthen your time-management skills. As an employee, you have a set schedule and get used to clocking in and out at a certain time each workday. This schedule/system is not quite the same for an entrepreneur. You will definitely work more hours and work harder then you ever did for anyone else (especially in the beginning,) so you have to be ready to *create* your work schedule and plan what a typical day will look like. Stick to the schedule just like you would at a regular job. This will help with productivity and consistency.

No job will be too big or small! As an employee, you can count on team members and third-party entities to help market, ful-fill orders, create analysis reports, answer phones, assist with customer service and even clean the toilets. But when you are first starting off, you will do it all if you don't have the resources to hire! Be prepared to do it all.

CHAPTER 10

Your multiple streams of income

Never Depend on a single income.
Make Investments to create a second
income. -Warren Buffet

I have to admit, this is by far the hardest chapter I have had to write in this book. Although each of my streams of income occurred organically, there have been many times throughout my Beautyprenuer journey that I beat myself up for diversifying my business too quickly. But in the end, it has actually saved me and is still keeping my doors open at this very moment.

In 2013 during my ideation phase, I only dreamt about developing a product line that would make millions and sell all over the world in retail stores. That is where my focus was. In 2016 when I launched my line, I continued to keep that focus and worked solely on the development of the products. At this point I had been a practicing medical aesthetics practitioner for more than six years, so I knew the service portion of the med spa very well. But I wanted to get my product sales off the ground, first. After about two years of working with the products, the need for the beauty educational services was overwhelming, so I decided to take my service experiences and develop my academy curriculum.

I started teaching my academy classes at small "boutique" hotels so I could create an intimate learning environment for my students, I had to have a separate teaching space because at the time, my services were rendered at a spa where I rented a room. My products were 95% B2B (business to business) and e-commerce sales, so there was no need for my own brick and mortar spa. The room I rented was more than sufficient. The moment that we started offering the classes, they grew popular and became a large part of my focus. I began teaching the classes nationally and within a year, I saw the need to open a spa and training facility. I created the facility with the idea that I would have a consistent space to teach academy classes, and my graduating students would have a place to service their clients.

Within three and a half years' time, I went from having a product company to having a product, beauty training, and spa business. As I am writing this book, we are in the middle of a pandemic, and my spa is mandatorily closed for safety reasons. The spa services income was instantly impacted by this. My academy classes also became limited for safety reasons, and out-of-town teaching opportunities had to be cancelled. But guess what? The online product orders have more than tripled!!!

What if the opposite happened, and the internet crashed for two days leaving me incapable of taking online orders? I could still pivot and focus on marketing the spa and classes.

I say all of that to say, your goal should be to have income coming from both offline and online customer bases as an entrepreneur. You should always be creating multiple streams of income. You should initially start with one thing that you do well - a product or service that you are "known" for - and then gradually expand your offering to keep your customers coming back for more. They will always want the "new" and "exciting" things that you offer if you develop long-term relationships with them.

Here are a few ways to easily diversify your income after you come up with your initial product or service:

- Book paid speaking gigs on your business journey or niche.
- Book consulting gigs at companies and corporations in your industry.
- Create an E-book.
- Start a podcast to increase engagement and promote sales.
- If you are selling a product, you can incorporate a related service. Do the same if you are selling a service, incorporate a product to sale with it.
- Create memberships or subscriptions around your product or service.
- Create trainings or teach subjects related to your niche.

$\mathcal{Y}$our Systems

When starting your Beautyprenuer journey, you should always start it off right. In my organization, **SYSTEMS** stand for **Saves You Stress Time Energy & Money.**

As you launch your business, there are five essential **SYSTEMS** I recommend you put in place.

1. Email Marketing and Customer Management System

There are several different systems from which to choose. Depending on what you are selling, some will work better than others. My top five picks are the following:

- Mailchimp
- Constant contact
- Convertkit
- Active Campaign

2. Lead page system

In digital marketing, a landing page is a standalone web page, created specifically for a marketing or advertising campaign. It's where a visitor "lands" after they click on a link in an email, or ads from Google, YouTube, Facebook, Instagram, Twitter, or similar places on the web.

Unlike websites, which typically have many goals and encourage exploration, landing pages are designed with a single focus or goal, known as a call to action (or CTA, for short). For example, if I run an ad for a military audience and another one for moms who shave, I do not want them going to the same web page. They will go to different pages with words that relate to their specific needs. The same would go for a stylist who advertises to someone with "natural hair" vs "relaxed or straightened hair." Their landing pages will be different because they will buy different types of products.

You need to be able to build landing pages, so you can generate income from the campaigns that you offer. You will need a different page for each audience, so I suggest using one of the following 3 resources below to create your landing pages.

These 3 platforms are designed for adding drop and drag text and images onto your web pages. These are easy for you to build yourself but of course, come with a monthly cost, so the alternative to these platforms is having a web designer create individual pages on a WordPress site for you. Here are the sites you can use:

- Clickfunnels
- Leadpages
- Kajabi

3. Scheduling Service (for the service-based businesses)

As a service provider you should have an efficient tool for your clients to book appointments with you that also helps to make your life easier. These systems should send your clients automatic appointment reminders, collect appointment deposits, process recurring fees and offer any other functions you need to efficiently run your business. My top five recommendations are the following:

- Acuity
- Mindbody
- Styleseat
- Glossgenius
- Booksy

4. Inventory System (for physical products)

It's extremely important to keep track of what you have on-hand and what you need to order. With an inventory system in place, you and your clients will never have to worry about items being out of stock, and you will not have to deal with fulfilment delays! As a small business, inventory management helps to prevent stock outages, manage multiple locations, and ensure accurate recordkeeping. An inventory system can save time and make the process much easier than doing it manually.

Here are some of the sites you can use (Your website may also have an inventory function):

- Boxstorm
- Netsuite
- Xero
- Squareup

5. Accounting Software

Track your money! If you're like me, you are not an accountant, and the thought of putting together a balance sheet probably induces a headache! So, when you're starting your business and can't afford an accountant, you need to have an accounting software in place that can be connected to your bank accounts and do most of the heavy lifting for you! There are several available options and depending on your specific accounting needs, you will need to determine which software works best for you. Here are some of the top services I recommend:

- QuickBooks
- Xero
- Freshbooks
- Wave Accounting

CHAPTER 12

*Y*our Client Experience

No matter what you are selling, product or service, customer service excellence should always a top priority! When a client purchases from you, everything about that experience should leave a positive impact on them. If you are a service provider, the environment where you provide the service should make your client feel a certain way. Decide what that *feeling* is and set the stage to make it happen. Do you want your client to have a relaxing experience or are you the "Southwest" of haircare and provide a "party" atmosphere with margaritas and lots of laughs? That decision is up to you.

If you are a product provider on the other hand, that experience starts at your website or vendor setup and ends with the "fancy pink box" that arrives at the door. Make sure your client knows that you appreciate them for making the purchase. You can include a handwritten thank-you card or a coupon/gift with each order. I once ordered a dress from an online boutique that gives a free, high-quality T-shirt with each order. While

I may have worn that dress two or three times, I have always remembered the shirt and still wear it years later. It's the little things that count and go a long way towards building long-term client relationships.

Some examples of things to do for client retention would be:

- **Free service add-ons.** If they get a massage, offer aromatherapy or a free foot scrub.
- **Free samples**. If clients purchase a product, give them a small sample of another product.
- **Referral Rewards.** If a client refers someone to you, offer them a discount or some sort of reward for that referral.
- **Loyalty Rewards**. I personally give any client that orders more than three times a loyalty discount, and it works very well! For services, if a client buys a package of three or more, they get one free service added on or one retail product. Customize it based on what you offer.
- **Use subscriptions and memberships to enhance customer experiences.** If I know that I'm getting 30% or more off a consistent product at a great discount every month, I would be more likely to buy membership.
- **Thank your customers.** Handwritten notes are always a hit!
- **Apologize for mistakes.** If something is damaged during shipment, replace it without question and offer a discount for the next order.

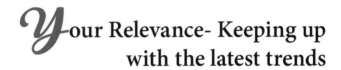

CHAPTER 13

*Y*our Relevance- Keeping up with the latest trends

Becoming and staying relevant in your industry is an important part of any business but shouldn't be the only focus. You need to be aware of trends in your industry to incorporate them, but you don't need to chase every new trend in the business. For example, the hair industry is ever-changing. If you are a stylist and the hair coloring trend goes from highlights to ombre to balayage coloring, you need to be aware of that so that you have the skills to keep up if your customers are asking for it. If you are a makeup artist who doesn't know how to contour, that may be a problem for you considering this is something very common in makeup practices today.

Some of the industry trends may be easy to incorporate and can help you to increase your revenue, so stay aware of what is going on around you and use the opportunity to capitalize on it when you can.

A perfect example of this would be Tito's Vodka, who is now making hand sanitizer during this COVID-19 pandemic.

A viral video was all it took. A lady went on YouTube and mistakenly told the world to use Tito's Vodka as a hand sanitizer during the pandemic. Tito's initially responded by telling peo-ple it wasn't true because their products didn't meet the 70% alcohol requirement set by the CDC. However, it was too late, the story was already out there, so they rose to the occasion. One week later, they were suddenly thrust into the sanitizer industry! Another example is a beer company I follow on Facebook. They saw the Popeye's Chicken sandwich craze unfold and decided that they would begin a marketing campaign that says "Our beer pairs perfectly with Popeye's chicken sandwich." This was a perfect trend-inspired marketing campaign. How can you take your product or service and tie it into one of the latest beauty trends? Our company uses aloe gel for a few of our products. When the COVID-19 pandemic hit, I had 50 pounds of aloe in my storage. So guess what new product Camellia Alise began manufacturing? Hand sanitizer in our signature scents! We sold out of our first batch in 5 days.

Keep in mind that you have to watch trends nationally and regionally because the service industry tends to update regionally, and the product industry tends to be more nationally updated. Although if you are working with a big box retailer, the stores favor regional trends.

$\mathcal{Y}$our Leadership

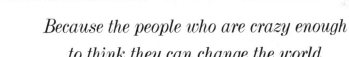

*Because the people who are crazy enough
to think they can change the world
are the ones who do. -Steve Jobs*

Within the past 13 chapters, we have gone over all the foundational tools needed to successfully launch your endeavor. You have the power to be successful at anything you put your mind and your energy into. What truly sets those who succeed apart from those who don't? The truth is, it is all about the mindset you have. An amazing speaker and mentor Jonathon Sprinkles recently reminded me that if one failure can easily defer someone's dreams, then they were not really in it and destined for success in the first place. There will be so many moments of failures and moments where you will feel stuck, but you must overcome them. Here is where the first **"E"** comes into play.

Eliminate excuses. Your excuses will always hold you back from reaching your full potential. There will always be a problem that can cause you to stand still or "give up." You have to make the choice to persevere and continue fighting to achieve success. Any successful person can probably tell you at least 10 situations that made them want to give up, but they didn't. You must have a belief in yourself that no matter what happens, you will succeed and achieve your dreams. No one else can convince you that you can be successful if you don't believe it.

Your success will only be limited by the actions you take and the ones you don't, so stop focusing on reasons why you shouldn't take action. Let go of the mentality that "I will get to it later" or "Maybe now isn't the time" and hit the damn GO button!

Here are 5 actions you need to take right now to stop procrastination in its tracks!!!

- **Set a daily routine and schedule**. Keep yourself productive and moving. Each day, give yourself at least one small task to complete. One small thing to help move your business and personal life forward will make a world of a difference.
- **Pump yourself up!** Find a motivation tool that helps keep your energy up and keeps you motivated. Music, meditation, exercise, prayers, bubble baths, gratitude journals, or dancing are just a few ways to keep your

energy up, keep yourself grounded as well as keep you moving forward even in the hardest of moments.

- **Expand your knowledge.** I read an article that said billionaires read over 50 books per year. They never stop learning and always have a thirst for knowledge. The more you learn, the more confident you become in your skills.

- **Get rid of the negative influences**. It is perfectly okay and encouraged for you to cut people and situations out of your life if they are draining you of your energy and causing you to doubt yourself and your dreams. If they aren't adding to your life in a positive way, cut them out of your life. Successful people tend to associate with other successful people and feed off each other's energy in a good way.

- **Be stingy with your time.** The **number one distraction** and time drainer for me is social media! Have you ever found yourself endlessly scrolling for an hour thinking "I need to be doing something else" and then feel guilty for having wasted so much time? We believe that everyone on social media is doing "so much more" and "achieving so much more" than we are. In case you don't already know this, most of what we see on social media are carefully curated mirages of what people want you to see. Now I know you are thinking, "Didn't she just tell me to keep up with trends earlier?" Yes. Yes, I did. You need to use social media for business purposes, but make it part of the job, limit the amount of days and hours that you spend on there and have a specific reason to engage. Don't just aimlessly scroll for hours without a purpose. This bad habit will give more excuses not to move forward because "Everyone else is already doing what you are trying to do, right?" Don't believe the hype! The **second time drainer** for me is other people, there will always be people who want to pick your brain for one reason or another, or vent, or socialize with you but if you are trying to reach certain goals you have to use your time strategically and not allow others to manipulate your time and energy because this can always be an easy way to lose track of your time. If your "work day" as an entrepreneur is 9am - 5pm treat your time as valuable and operate your day with those parameters.

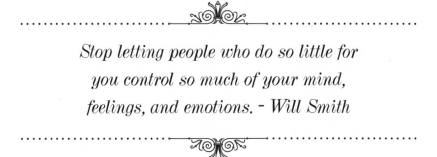

Stop letting people who do so little for you control so much of your mind, feelings, and emotions. - Will Smith

The second "E" of the leadership pillars is to **Execute Effectively**.

This entire book has been about how to successfully launch your Beautyprenuer journey and putting together the plan to execute that launch but planning without action is useless. You have to do both. So here is the list for taking all the plans and goals you have set and putting action behind them to achieve the success you desire and deserve!

- Have clear and aligned goals throughout the organization.
- Have a work/life routine or schedule to which you can hold yourself accountable.
- Develop a strong mission and vision statement.
- Create a set of core values and company culture aspects to impart upon your future team.
- Establish a weekly tracking system. All goals should be updated and assessed regularly by you and your leadership and/or mentor.
- Establish your strategic objectives for the month and quarter and clarify exactly what needs to be executed.
- Set up a process to close out and review all goals at quarter-end, using insight from each quarter to set the next quarter's goals.

I can never be safe; I always try and go against the grain. As soon as I accomplish one thing, I just set a higher goal. That's how I've gotten to where I am. - Beyonce

The third "E" and final pillar of my leadership program has always been to **enhance your enterprise by monetizing**

your expertise and experience. I believe we all have special skills and natural abilities. If you are extremely new to your industry, then I don't recommend teaching right away because your experiences and your stories become the most valuable part of the teaching experience. But if you are launching your Beautyprenuer journey as a way to enhance a skill you have already mastered; I wholeheartedly believe you should add a teaching component to your business. For example, if you are a hairstylist who has been doing hair for 20 years and you are about to create your own hair product, why not work on the development of your product and create a workshop on healthy hair? This is a great way to launch the new haircare brand! There are various ways to pair your expertise with a teaching component, but it will take a little time for you to strategize and figure out the right way to pair them.

Build a good relationship with your audience before monetizing. The audience is more likely to engage with you and spend money if they feel that your goal is to offer value.

Six Means to Monetize Your Expertise:

- **Digital Resources.** Think about checklists, worksheets, workbooks, and other resources you can create from your existing content. Clients will pay to download something that solves a specific problem for them.
- **Write a book.** Translate your knowledge into a book. Find your niche subject and a select a theme to educate your audience on based on the valuable experiences

you have already had. Organize the content, choose a publishing method, and sell it. You can make a downloadable e-book, use a self-publishing system, find a publishing house, or create an audiobook.

- **Workshops and Seminars.** Offer your expertise to an audience as another way to monetize your knowledge. Initially, you may want to give some free workshops to build credibility and add to your resumé. After you've gotten some experience in making presentations and you've built up your confidence, you can work with events that pay presenters or organize your own seminars as paid events. (If you have no presentation experience, you might want to strengthen your skills with Toastmasters or other local public speaking groups for practice first.)

- **Online Courses.** One of the most effective ways to monetize your expertise is to offer paid webinars to your subscribers or to a target audience. Once you know what you want to teach, you can utilize online platforms such as Zoom, Udemy, or Teachable to capitalize on the opportunity to earn money by offering video courses.

- **Sponsored Posts and E-mails.** When you build enough influence that you are sought out for your knowledge or a company seeks access to your target audience, they will pay you for it. Begin to write guest posts on blogs, online publications, social media accounts, or e-mail newsletters. This is basically an advertorial.

- **Subscription.** If your content is developed and you have built a following and loyal audience, building a membership or subscription portal is a great way to monetize your knowledge and expertise. People are willing to pay a monthly fee for recurring content that is valuable. This is common for training tools, podcasts, and mastermind groups.

Monetize your expertise by sharing your knowledge with a target audience. Building that audience allows you to create revenue for the work you are already doing. Less work for more money.

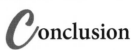

CHAPTER 15

*C*onclusion

S tarting your Beautyprenuer journey won't be easy, and the journey will be unique, as no two journeys are alike. Some days will be amazing, and some will be difficult. But if you have a passion, a purpose, dedication, and an execution plan, you can be successful in this industry. New product and service companies are launching every day in this 7-billion-dollar industry. And just like me, you can capitalize on the opportunity. At the core, you have to remember your *why* for what you are doing and keep yourself motivated.

How far can you go if you stop procrastinating, take the principles presented in this book and get started? Eliminate the excuses and take one step forward toward success every day.

Success is a decision and built on actions. It is not a gift , an entitlement, or based on luck. You have to work for success and to achieve your dreams. Now that you are primed and ready to go out there and get it, MAKE IT HAPPEN! Choose success, take what you want, ask for what you need and stop at nothing until you get it.

Think about it this way, 10% of the richest people in the United States own almost 70% of the country's total wealth. To do "extraordinary" things and rise to the top, you have to be willing to walk away from the actions and habits of the 90% and create your own pathway to wealth and success.

Most importantly, let your journey be an organic evolution! And again, congratulations on taking the steps to reaching your goals. Reach out to my team anytime at sales@camelliaalise.com if you want more information. Thank you for reading and remember...

"Speak what you seek until
you see what you said."

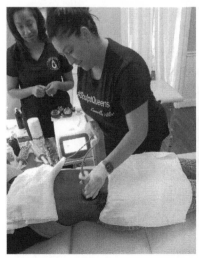

CHAPTER 16

Worksheets & Resources

On the following pages you will find all the resources previously listed, summarized for your usage and I have also included 2 goal setting worksheets to help you along the way!

I also included a few really great resources that I didn't list previously, as a bonus. I hope these resources are equally useful in arming you with the tools you need to successfully launch your Beautyprenuer journey.

Daily Success Habit Worksheet

We often overlook the **IMPORTANCE** of **DAILY HABITS** in managing ourselves and our lives. But, it's often by making small changes to our daily routine that we make **BIG** changes in our lives or careers!

MY TOP 3 PRIORITIES IN LIFE RIGHT NOW ARE:

1. .... 2. .... 3. ....

MY TOP 3 STRESSORS IN LIFE RIGHT NOW ARE:

1. .... 2. .... 3. ....

WHAT SUPPORTIVE DAILY HABITS WILL YOU INTRODUCE?

THEY MUST BE SPECIFIC AND MEASURABLE SO YOU KNOW EXACTLY WHAT TO DO, AND CAN CLEARLY SAY YOU HAVE COMPLETED THE STEP! SEE EXAMPLES BELOW:

- Have 15 minutes of silence or alone time each day
- Drink 8 glasses of water a day
- Be at my desk by 8.00am/leave by 6.00pm every day
- Eat a healthy breakfast every morning
- Make all my calls in the first hour of the day
- Write my top 3 tasks for the day before starting work
- Connect daily with partner/spouse (5 mins listening)

1 -

2 -

3 -

4 -

5 -

HOW ARE YOU GOING TO IMPLEMENT THESE HABITS? I WILL COMMIT TO THESE HABITS BY:

I WILL IMPLEMENT THESE HABITS ON: .... *(SPECIFIC DATE WHEN YOU WILL START)*

WHO DO I NEED TO BE TO IMPLEMENT THESE HABITS? I WILL BE SOMEONE WHO IS:

1. .... 2. .... 3. ....

Goal Worksheet

PRIORITY GOALS	DEADLINES
1 -	
2 -	
3 -	
4 -	
5 -	

GOALS & ASPIRATIONS
WHO DO YOU ASPIRE TO BE? WHERE DO YOU WANT TO GO?

PERSONAL GOAL EXAMPLES:

- I will finish beauty school by: .... (specific deadline to finish)
- I will launch my business by: .... (specific deadline to launch)
- I will save $.......................... by: .... (specific deadline to reach goal)

BUSINESS GOAL EXAMPLES:

- I will finish my ingredient deck by: .... (specific deadline to finish)
- I will have inventory in stock by: .... (specific deadline to reach goal)
- I will launch my website by: .... (specific deadline to reach goal)
- I will have .... monthly service clients by: .... (specific deadline to reach goal)
- I will have ....people on my email list by:............................ (specific deadline to reach goal)

CONSISTENTLY DO A MENTAL CHECK, ASK YOURSELF:

- Are you working as hard as you can to achieve these goals?
- Are you doing something everyday to move you towards these goals?
- What can you do better? How will you improve?
- Have you honestly been giving your all to meet your goals?
- What have you done lately that has made you proud?

RESOURCE INDEX

PRIVATE LABEL SUPPLIERS

- Wholesalesupplyplus.com
- Wholesalenaturalbodycare.com
- Essentialwholesale.com
- Sourcevital.com

CUSTOM FORMULATION CLASSES

- Formulabotanica.com
- Smartmajority.com
- Schoolofnaturalskincare.com

CUSTOM FORMULA INGREDIENTS

- Newdirectionsaromatics.com
- Bathbodysupply.com
- Texasnaturalsupply.com
- Brambleberry.com

CUSTOM FORMULA MANUFACTURERS

- Mseedgroup.com
- Texasbeautylabs.com
- Rainshadowlabs.com

WEBSITE PLATFORMS

- Wix
- Shopify
- Magento
- Wordpress

SEO PLATFORMS

- Google
- Yelp
- Amazon
- Etsy
- Social media platforms

GRAPHIC DESIGNERS/ INTERNATIONAL WORKFORCE

- Upwork.com
- Fiverr.com
- Peoplebythehour.com

CUSTOMER FEEDBACK/SURVEY COMPANY

- Jotform.com
- Surveymonkey.com
- Google docs

SOCIAL MEDIA TOOLS

- IQ Hashtags
- Planoly
- Later.com
- Hootsuite
- Buffer

EMPLOYEE PERSONALITY TEST

- 16personalities.com

BUSINESS PLAN TEMPLATES

- Bplans.com
- Sba.gov
- Profitableventure.com/beauty-salon-business-plan/
- Score.org

CROWDFUNDING PLATFORMS

- Ifundwomen
- Kickstarter
- Indigogo
- NextSeed

BUSINESS PITCH COMPETITIONS

- New Voices Fund competition

- Houston Liftoff competition
- HCC business plan competition
- Next Seed Female Founders competition
- Bank of America competition
- BBVA Compass competition
- Cricket Wireless competition
- HMSDC, Houston Minority Supplier Development Council competition

GRANT PROGRAM RESOURCES

- Grants.gov
- Grantsourceapp.com
- Challenge.gov
- Grantwatch.com
- Local and industry-related organizations

SMALL BUSINESS LENDERS

- Trufund
- Peopefund
- Liftfund

EMAIL MARKETING & CUSTOMER MANAGEMENT SYSTEMS

- Mailchimp
- Constant contact
- Convertkit

- Active Campaign

LEAD PAGE COMPANIES

- Clickfunnels
- Leadpages
- Kajabi

SCHEDULING SYSTEMS

- Acuity
- Mindbody
- Styleseat
- Glossgenius
- Booksy

INVENTORY SYSTEMS

- Boxstorm
- Netsuite
- Xero
- Squareup

ACCOUNTING SOFTWARE

- QuickBooks
- Xero
- Freshbooks
- Wave Accounting

ONLINE TEACHING PLATFORMS

- Thinkific
- CourseCraft
- OpenLearning
- Skillshare
- Teachable
- Udemy

FREE STOCK PHOTOS

- Burst by Shopify
- Createherstock
- Deposit Photos
- Free Nature Stock
- Gratisography
- Pixabay
- StockSnap
- Unsplash

Made in the USA
Monee, IL
18 January 2022

89194784R00065